Changing Lives Forever

Psychoruptcy

It's Worse Than Bankruptcy!

We need to budget our psychological resources as we do with our financial resources

This book is created with you in mind

Dr Sammad T Hashmi
Psychiatrist

Editing and graphics by Lisa Melian

ISBN: 979-8-8486-3391-7

YouTube Channel: Dr Hashmi Online
Facebook: Dr Hashmi Online
Instagram: drhashmionline

REMEMBER

You are the finest creation of the universe

Value yourself!

Psychoruptcy

CONTENTS

Psychoruptcy

ACKNOWLEDGMENTS

To the readers, as you have taken the first step to becoming psychomillionaires.

To my wonderful wife Yanesha and absolutely fantastic boys Harris and Zain.

Psychoruptcy

INTRODUCTION

We live in a complex world of information overload. Our psychological resources are constantly under various pressures from our inner and outer systems and events. Many of them are beyond our control, for example we do not choose our parents, biological relations and of course, childhood events. We have no control over our lives in a real sense but virtually, we like to believe we do. This brings about an incoherence within our own systems and psychological processes.

As individuals we are unique; we have different personalities, life values and perceptions of others and the world around us. Our experience is exclusive to each of us and therefore unequivocal, which is excellent on the one hand but challenging on the other. Consequently, we must manage our minds in a way that is unique to anyone else in the big wide world.

Similarly, our psychological resources are very individual as well. We all have a different set of abilities and are expected to use our strengths and weaknesses to navigate through life as best we can. However, some of us find it extraordinarily challenging to use the resources. This is not because we were not awarded the resources by nature, but more that we are unaware of the extent of our abilities and how to utilise them efficiently. It is not dissimilar to someone who has a healthy bank account but who lacks awareness of it and its true value or moreover, they struggle to work out how to invest the resource to get the optimum reward from it.

Enter the concept of psychological budgeting. Very much like financial resource budgeting, we need psychological resource budgeting to avoid the trap of negative equity (financial and psychological respectively). The end goal is to avoid facing psychoruptcy, which is much worse than bankruptcy!

This book is all about psychological budgeting; the ways we can estimate our resources, methods we can apply to budget and most importantly, how to avoid psychoruptcy- a *deadly* state of mind!

The Concept

In purely financial terms, we all get paid a set amount of money with fixed intervals in between- a monthly wage. This is our allocated financial resource. We are expected to live within our means and to save some money for rainy days. The financial resource is very individual and lies on a large spectrum, with some people earning more than others.

Let's look at an example. In a typical household, expenses fall under three main categories. Firstly, there are always permanent and fixed expenses that must be paid, whether we like it or not. The second set of expenses includes variable spending such as utility bills, which are directly proportional to a family's use of any specific utility. The purchase of food, clothes, travel and any planned or unplanned social activities are also considered as variable. The third set comprises of unexpected and unplanned spending, beyond and outside usual daily living; this may include out of the blue repairs for the car or if the washing machine breaks down and needs replacing. In an ideal situation, families always aim to live within their means and to keep room for financial maneuvers for all fixed, variable, and unexpected expenses. In the real world, this rarely happens. Over the years, we have learned to live on loans and undue reliance on credit cards hence, many of us are stuck in a life of debt despite earning a decent wage. As the saying goes 'the more we earn, the more we spend'.

Before going any further and describing the real financial

framework of a household, let us compare and apply similar principles to our psychological resources. The key difference is that we are paid a wage at variable intervals, ranging from daily to every four weeks, depending on the type of work we do and whether we are employed or self-employed. Usually most of us are paid each month, which tends to be the most common interval between our financial resource allocation. The psychological resource (psychoresource), however, works on a fixed interval of daily allocation, which is set each morning when we wake up. The *quality* of the resources available for the day is important. If we have woken up after a decent sleep, it is likely that our psychoresource is in better shape. If we have woken up in a positive mood and emotional state, and in a stable environment, then of course we have far more psychological resource to spend during the day. In these circumstances, we are better prepared to deal with day-to-day psychological inconveniences without feeling drained or overwhelmed.

Each day our psychoresource may be used to fund three familiar categories of spending: fixed psychological resource spending, variable psychological resource spending and emergency psychological resource spending. Like financial debt, if we are not careful, we can very easily slip into psychological debt (psychodebt). Once we get trapped in the cycle of psychodebt, it is extremely hard to pull ourselves out and reach a place of balance.

Balance Comparison

It is hard to pull ourselves out of financial debt, but it is many times harder to pull ourselves out of psychological debt! To overcome financial debt, we need to keep the books balanced throughout life, but for many this is a challenging task. We need to act like a good financial manager and sometimes we need help from financial experts to balance our books. An increase in wage is always helpful but quite often we are required to take on extra work to increase our income. On rare occasions, we get blessed with a bag of money from an unexpected (or expected) source, either by winning the lottery or through inheritance. We all find this unexpected pot of money useful and sometimes, essential to pull us out of the financial debt trap.

Similarly, to get out of psychological debt traps we are expected to work harder, accept professional assistance, find an additional source to increase our psychological resource and most importantly, we need effective psychoresource budgeting. Coupled with your commitment and effort, this book will provide you with the motivation and guidance to balance the psychofiscal books. The alternative is to spend life in constant psychological debt with little chance of feeling happy or content.

The Psychobank

At this stage it is essential to grasp the concept of psychobank. The psychobank is similar to a high street bank in that it offers a current account, a savings account, short and long-term investments and short and long-term loans in the same way a high street bank does but instead of dealing with hard cash, it manages psychocurrency.

What is psychocurrency? At the centre of it lies emotional and mental strength and resilience. These often stem from the loving, nurturing, supportive relationships we experience with the special people in our lives such as our families, friends, close work colleagues and partners. The love, support and reassurance we gain from these important attachments in our lives, we internalise and use to strengthen our psychocurrency, enabling us to afford our day-to-day spending.

Other sources of psychocurrency include: our mental priorities, our acts of kindness which bring satisfaction, our personal possessions which we spend years acquiring, particularly those that hold sentimental value. Our intellectual state and spiritual well-being (including concepts such as self-realisation) also form part of this phenomenon. These sources of psychocurrency are highly individual and unique, varying from person to person.

The savings account is primarily linked with our biological relationships, namely our parents and siblings, whom we might not see on a daily basis, but who we can rely on when in need of extra love and support to replenish our psychocurrency. It is almost like our default setting. Let's consider examples of how our current and savings accounts operate. Imagine returning home after an exceedingly hard day to a welcoming, supportive spouse and houschold or mccting a trusted friend or close colleague after work. These positive interactions serve to make you feel better and strengthen your emotional well-being. Essentially you have dipped into your current account to replenish your psychocurrency. In contrast, imagine you are struggling to cope with a home environment that is no longer welcoming, or maybe your relationship is on the verge of breakdown, meeting a friend or a work colleague might not be as conducive to replenishing your psychocurrency. You are more likely to resort to seeking comfort from the unconditional love and non-judgemental support offered by parents or siblings. In doing so you are accessing your savings account to balance the books, which is slightly more reliable and secure. Often by default we seek comfort from people we trust, who accept us the way we are and who understand us.

There are times when just being in a familiar, safe environment is enough to generate satisfactory funds for the psychobank to avoid an overdraft.

Now let's take a look at psychoinvestments. As with high street banks, investments can be for short, medium and long-term. Short-term psychoinvestments refer to superficial sources that people rely on to briefly and quickly increase their psychocurrency, for example retail therapy brings emotional relief for some, albeit momentary. Others may accumulate possessions, which can lead to hoarding. The psychological gain is time-limited and surface-level; it tends to keep us afloat through a brief crisis. Short term psychoinvestment fails to safeguard against major adverse life events. Consider a relationship breakdown, the value of an item that once brought momentary happiness, is now insignificant.

Medium-term psychoinvestments have a greater and longer-lasting impact on our inner worlds and therefore our psychocurrency. Examples include our values, positive relationships we build over time, trust we install, emotions we invest in pets and the lives we feel responsible for nurturing as well as memories we like to revisit. These investments are excellent at cushioning us from serious life events such as loss, grief, illness, and disability, but as always, these investments are limited in supply. If an individual experiences trauma for an extended period of time, medium-term investment is gradually depleted, and the individual is left at risk of psychodebt.

Long-term infinite investments enhance our spirituality, which lies at the core of our being. Imagine for a second, a psychocurrency printing machine installed inside each of us to provide strength and unlimited resources to meet the constant demand placed on our psychobank accounts. To install the psychocurrency printing machine a certain level of spiritual awareness must be achieved, which is a challenging task that requires concerted effort over many years. A state of true contentment is enjoyed when our inner and outer worlds align.

Psycholoans

In an ideal world, we would all have substantial psychocurrency available to spend, but in reality, we are not always this fortunate. Some of us simply do not have enough psychocurrency to save and must rely on loans to cope when crisis hits.

Psycholoans are similar to financial loans from any lender, whether a commercial or private bank and involves psychocredit with high interest rate. The loans can be for the short-term or long-term (like our life-time mortgages).

Let's explore how psycholoans work. If our savings account is empty, then one may desperately opt for risky psycholoans in the form of alcohol or drug dependency. Individuals find themselves relying on these recreational substances to feel more in control and to gain a false sense of psychoenergy. These types of psycholoans are often dangerous and damaging with a high interest rate that becomes extremely expensive for our psychological systems to afford in the long-term.

Psychowaste

Being wasteful can drain our savings whether in the form of hard cash or psychocurrency. Protecting our psychosavings from waste is an invaluable skill.

Economically speaking, it is easy to understand the many ways in which we are wasteful with our financial resource, our money. However, in terms of our psychological resource and our psychobank it is a harder concept to grasp. Our psychosavings are easily consumed by jealousy, revenge, hatred, arrogance and similar negative feelings. It is impossible to build a healthy psychoaccount based on these when psychocurrency stems from love, trust, care and support. We must therefore be mindful about our attitude and behaviour since these are key players in determining whether we are psychologically wasteful or protective.

Psychoresource Allocation and Management

Psychological debt management can be a harder concept to grasp than financial debt management due to several reasons. Firstly, psychological resource calculation and allocation are based on a fixed daily principle; this short 24-hour interval means there is little room for maneuvering resources hence daily effort is needed in all spending areas. We are usually allocated psychological resources for the day when we wake up each morning. Secondly, the obscure nature of psychodebt makes it difficult to even estimate the allocated quantity. In essence, if we don't know the amount or scale of our resource, how can we even consider any form of budgeting? In contrast, money is tangible; we can touch it, withdraw cash from a machine and look at bank statements. This is not the case with psychological resources- we don't have this advantage- but we can feel it at emotional level. Hence, the difference between financial resource and debt and psychological resource and debt is a matter of one being real and the other, virtual. The former is linked with external factors and perception whilst the latter, with internal factors and feelings and emotions. The third issue is that when dealing with financial resource, its physical presence is satisfactory but psychological resource management involves dealing with your mind, an entity that can be quite unfriendly at times.

Before further discussing resource allocation and debt management, it is essential for us to understand what the mind is.

Brain Versus Mind

It is important to differentiate between the brain and mind. The brain is our friend; it provides us with all the right resources and works in coordination with our bodies to keep us functioning. In contrast, our mind acts as a military-styled dictator who has taken power by force to use our 'brainy' resources. We need to work with our brain to fight a battle against our mind.

Our mind is extraordinarily lazy and extremely controlling. You can appreciate the extent of its laziness by the fact that in our life spans, we are lucky if we manage to use a small proportion of its capacity. Compare this with every other organ in your body, which on occasion can be abused by us to the extent that we end up wearing them out; our knees give way, our vision gets blurry, lung capacity is reduced and the heart struggles to beat- but we continue to use them until one of them fails and refuses to function beyond demand. Now compare this with the mind; it does not allow us to make sense of many things we encounter in life. It keeps us trapped in our past by showing us old reels of films and movies of our lives- nothing new, nothing creative. It convinces us that this is our reality, and we deserve no better. It leaves you feeling helpless, like you have no sense of control. This is why it is difficult to manage psychodebt; our mind gets in our way. Even when we are fully motivated and capable, we feel shaken by the mere thought of confronting or challenging our mind.

Psychoresource Calculation and Taxation

Before going into the specifics of psychoresource calculation and budgeting, we must remind ourselves that our financial resource comes with obligatory taxes of various kinds. We are employed, our tax is deducted at base. If we are self-employed or in business, we must pay tax based on our earnings; this is something we cannot avoid. When it comes to our mind, which is lazy and the most controlling organ in the body, tax is brutally deducted from our psychoresource with no opportunity to appeal and no concept of justice. If our mind has decided to set us up for failure, we have a real battle on our hands. The question arises; how does our mind calculate the amount of tax we have to pay on our psychoresource? In short, our psychoresource is taxed at the base and the remainder given to us to utilise, which is what we wake up with each morning. This is a simple concept that is easy to understand. We should presume that each of us wakes up with 100%

pre-tax psychoresource, since we are all born with the potential to achieve the maximum; we are all born to lead content lives and to make the world a better place. We are all born to overcome disparities between our persona and real self and to achieve absolute psychological harmony with our true inner selves. We are all born to experience a life of happiness and peace- but this is rarely the reality.

Irrespective of the fact that we are born with huge potential, the contracts we sign with the world are different. We are tied down to our genetics. Following our entry into this world, we spend our early years having no control and being dependent on others around us. I am talking about the era of our life when even our brain is oblivious to the idea of controlling us. By the time we acquire physical independence, the water has already passed under the bridge. Brick by brick, layer by layer the foundations of our personality have already been laid. Our brain has already taken a beating prior to realising its own power and ability to control.

Consider the idea that our psychoresource allocation is 100% every morning. To establish the value of take-home resource we need to know the percentage the mind deducts at the base. In real financial terms, the more you earn, the more tax you pay. In psychological terms, the more emotional baggage you have from the past, the more heavily you will be taxed. Despite our mind being in a position of absolute control and its ruthlessness at deducting tax on our past and present adversities, it also works by principle of survival. If we did not exist, the mind would not exist; its existence is subject to our existence, hence the mind cannot apply 100% tax. In other words, the mind cannot claim all of our psychoresource as tax, leaving us with nothing to live on. The mind works according to the principle of proportionality; that is, the more adverse an event, the greater the tax value. This is a very individual calculation that cannot be generalized. It requires us to work through a process at the end of which we will have established the percentage to be deducted from our psychoresource, by our mind before allocation.

At this stage, we have understood the basic concept of our actual pre-taxed psychoresource allocation, principles that our mind applies to deduct tax, leaving us with the remainder of the take-home psychoresource to budget for fixed, variable, and unexpected psychological spending. We also understand that the process is highly individual and requires self-reflection. To facilitate the process, we need a psychoresource calculator.

Psychoresource Calculator

Using the psychoresource calculator is practical and mathematical with some degree of self-reflection. It is just a matter of practice for us to be able to master this skill. It simply involves drawing two columns on a sheet of paper and designating one column to *past* adverse events and the other to a value you would like to allocate to that specific event. This simple paper and pen exercise can also be repeated for *current* adverse events. The beauty of the psychoresource calculator is that anybody can use it at any point, there are no limits to its use or significance.

Try to prioritise the most significant events and avoid exceeding 3 events in any category (past or current). Being selective allows you to more easily identify root causes and underlying themes that shape your core thoughts and feelings. Often adverse events that we perceive as separate are linked and stem from the same root cause.

The first step we need to do is to complete the column labelled 'Past Adversities'. A lot of us live life carrying the weight of childhood adversities on our shoulders as unwanted baggage- but now we are going to allocate value to them. This column includes unfavorable personal experiences from over 12 months ago such as relationship breakdown, job loss, accidents, or loss of physical health. It could include past events that one perceives as negative from as far back as a young child. Value calculation is in numbers and hypothetically speaking, can range from 0-100 (although we have already established that the mind cannot tax an individual 100% of its psychoresource). Even a figure of 10% can be significant if viewed from a purely financial taxation system, when even a small rise is damaging. Bear in mind that everything cannot possibly be taxed, and the rule of rationality applies; this means that if we have experienced a difficult time or suffered a traumatic life event but at present, it is very much a memory and does not cause us a problem on a day-to-day basis, then the good news is that we will not be taxed. The reason being that on an emotional level, we have successfully recovered or healed emotionally from that stressful event and are not depleting our daily psychoresource by any means. On the other hand, any significant past events (from over 12 months ago) which continue to affect you and weigh you down emotionally on a day-to-day basis, is required to be taxed. A simple example is chronic ill health that may have started 5 years ago but is ongoing and continues to be an inconvenience, imposing restrictions on our daily function. Some physical health disorders that are well managed including diabetes or hypertension, may not satisfy the criteria because fortunately, a well-managed condition does not limit us.

The 'Current Adversities' column covers all present adversities and any events within the last 12 months that continue to have an impact, hence are ongoing. The section quite rightly includes ongoing social frictions, which may be from biological relatives, friends, or acquaintances. In other words, any ongoing family feud, non-ending divorce proceedings, issues with child access or establishing the lost links with someone significant, all apply here. This section can also include ongoing frictions within a household due to incompatible relationships.

Having reached the stage of identifying our taxable psychological events, to place a value on each, it is essential to go through the process of knowing-self. This is the most crucial part of psychoresource calculation because without knowing-self, we are likely to assign an incorrect value to the event and as a result, we either end up paying too much or too little psychological tax. Consequently, the take-home resource value will be incorrect and our resource allocation for fixed, variable, and unexpected psychological events will only lead to a psychoresource crisis. This carries the risk of psychoruptcy, leaving us with nothing to live on.

Knowing-Self

Let's take a moment to explore the process of knowing-self, which can help us estimate the tax value of a life event.

It is always beneficial to use words to describe oneself. The easiest way is to pick the first three words that come to mind, which represent oneself. These words will act as foundation blocks on which to build the process of knowing-self. There is a need to look at ourselves to establish whether we are influenced by others or whether we hold the power to influence others. Do we believe that we can change things around us, or do we believe things happen *to* us and we have little influence? Find your "Locus of Control": if it is internal then you are likely to believe that you do have control of aspects of your life and decision-making. On the other hand, if your locus of control is external, you are likely to believe that you have very little to no control over what happens. One can also reflect on whether they are an extrovert or an introvert.

An extrovert tends to be surrounded by a strong social support network which acts as a buffer against adverse life events, by way of diluting the severity of the impact of the event. This type of individual is likely to allocate less psychoresource to a life event, hence pay less tax, meaning more resources are available for spending.

An introvert tends to be isolative, preferring their own company. With little outside interference, these individuals tend to cope with adverse events independently and risk magnifying events. This is similar to catastrophizing, whereby one views a situation as considerably worse than it actually is. These individuals are therefore more likely to overpay tax, leaving themselves with less psychoresource to spend. Introverts also tend to be more cautious, which may not serve them well in exploring and achieving their full potential; they may never realise the full extent of the resources available. This is very much like someone who has money in their pocket but who fails to use it, wrongly believing that they do not have any.

Individuals who have a healthy mix of both extrovert and introvert traits are likely to rate a life event more realistically- if they manage to remain rational in terms of their emotions. These individuals are likely to be easily persuaded and they may welcome help in identifying and calculating how much tax they need to pay. However, this is dangerous because no one else can estimate an individual's self-perception of a life event nor its value to that individual; this process is extremely personal. There may be a select group of people who decide not to estimate the tax value for any life event because everything is so overwhelming for them. It is possible that they resort to putting a figure of 100% in front of every life event, believing that they are in absolute negative equity, with no right to achieve anything in life. They exclude all possibilities of change occurring. Although the numerical value for an event will eventually be their decision because of the extremely subjective nature of the process, persuasion, and encouragement by a loved one or a trusting partner will be required.

Within the process of knowing-self, there are other factors to be considered which could affect the self-perception of a life event, resulting in an individual either paying too much, or too little tax. Those who live a life of emotional uncertainty and who experience frequent extremes in emotion (either towards being happy or being depressed) are likely to place different values on an event at different times of the day, depending on the state of their mood. For this group it is wise to consider the old phrase that "truth is somewhere in the middle". The pessimists among us who live life wearing dark glasses with a tendency to see the glass half empty, are advised to divide the allocated value by two. In other words, halve it to compensate for the fact that the glass can also be viewed as half full and to balance their slightly skewed perception. In contrast, individuals who like to maintain a strong persona of success and happiness with a very high need for external approval, are unlikely to acknowledge the severity of the event and its true impact, unless this is done alone and in private because it is likely to damage their persona. A simple suggestion is that once this group of people assign a value to an event, simply multiply it by 2, double it. The same applies for the extreme optimists among us, to account for the fact the glass can be viewed as half empty as well and to balance their bias in thinking.

The Importance of Biological Functions

Another essential aspect of calculating psychological tax is our biological functions, the most identifiable of which include sleep, appetite, and desire for physical contact, usually known as libido. If there are no issues with biological function, then the influence of unfavorable past life events and current stresses is minimal, and one is likely to pay very little tax. This leaves greater psychoresource to spend, leading to a state of remarkable psychowealth.

The simplest method to reduce psychotax in terms of physiology, is to focus on naturally improving sleep and appetite, which will automatically reduce the burden on one's psychological systems and improve psyhocurrency for the day. The focus should be on diet and consuming superfoods whilst opting for a healthy lifestyle. A healthy sleep pattern is usually achieved by using techniques to block out blue light, for example the use of dark amber glasses prior to bedtime. Blocking the blue light activates the pineal gland, which once activated starts to secrete melatonin, a regulatory hormone to stabilize the sleep-wake cycle.

Psychoresource Modification Through Sleep

Sleep is a magical process that enhances the value of our psychoresource. It improves the availability of psychocurrency both in terms of quantity and quality.

The phases of sleep that are integral to improving our psychoresource include the very moment we fall asleep, when the brain moves from a state of full consciousness to unconsciousness and as we are waking up, when the brain transitions from unconsciousness to consciousness. If we learn how to best utilise these phases, we can become psychowealthy with little effort.

Mental preoccupation by a specific thought is a very powerful phenomenon. The thoughts we engage in as we drift off to sleep inform, what is referred to as *Information Feed*. This content is then processed by our brains and as a result we often experience dreams. The information then reappears at the other end as *Information Exit* on waking up.

We have very little influence over our dreams, and we are unable to directly control or shape the thoughts we have on waking up. However, we can deliberately influence the information we feed into our brain at the time of falling asleep, which in turn is likely to influence our dreams and the information that later elicits the thoughts we wake up with.

Let's look at a few examples that demonstrate this. Consider a student studying hard for an exam. He or she revises late into the night and falls asleep, book in hand and wakes up preoccupied by the thought of exams, which is anxiety provoking. It is very likely that the student's dreams would also have been associated with studying and exams, resulting in a far from restful sleep.

Imagine a property developer who is behind schedule on a renovation and is fearful of losing profit due to the delay. He or she is likely to invest a lot of mental energy thinking about ways to speed up the project. At night they lie awake troubleshooting ideas in their head, before finally falling asleep. It is likely that they wake up preoccupied by the same thoughts and that the content of their dreams shares a similar theme. Their quality of sleep is likely to be compromised. Poor sleep is damaging to the psychoresource.

We can learn to use the falling asleep phase to our advantage by intentionally controlling the thoughts that enter our information feed. Selecting and entertaining only those thoughts that are positive and helpful will be conducive towards retrieving thoughts of a similar nature during the information exit phase. As a result, we are very likely to wake up in the right state of mind and to have enjoyed a restful sleep.

Let's focus on what we *can* control and what we *can* do- we can choose the right information to feed in when falling asleep.

Valuing Life Events

Identifying the life events that have had an emotional impact on us is relatively simple but deciding the value to place on each event is more challenging. This may be due to an inherent fear of confronting reality or avoidance of any threat to their pre-existing psychological processes. It is likely that some of us may delay or postpone decision-making until the following day- and we all know, tomorrow never comes. For these individuals the suggestion is to use the principle of "half-half", which presumes that half of their psychoresource is taxed, and half is for them to budget for the day. This is the most realistic method one could apply to estimate the psychocurrency available for the day once tax has been deducted.

Some of us live a life of mistrust. Something "not quite right" is often the case. Amongst this group of people, there is a deep fear of something negative happening, leading to a state of constant mistrust of others and the world around them. This group may incorporate multiple past events into a single event that is then perceived as significant. They tend to identify every event as severe in nature and are unable to view their past and current life events realistically. The recommendation is simple; to follow the "half-half" rule. This is to balance out any catastrophizing.

For all those individuals who struggle to assign a realistic value to an event or who face difficulty identifying events, the rule of "half-half" seems realistic and applicable. In practical terms, whilst an allocation of 50% psychoresource (post-tax) for a day might not be correct for some, it is very realistic for many.

Virtually everyone is likely to be taxed by their mind between 40-60% of pre-taxed psychoresource, which is surprisingly substantial. This leaves the remainder of 40-60% psychoresource on waking up in the morning, to utilise for the day ahead. You may be tempted to adopt these figures as your own and skip the entire process of identifying your adverse past and present events and the taxes they incur. However, in doing so you lose the valuable opportunity to explore the core issues that are silently draining your own psychoresource. These are specific to you and knowing what they are is half the battle won- knowledge is power!

Spending Our Psychoresource

To recap, we have established that available psychoresource is very much like our income in financial terms, which is taxed from the base and subject to domestic budgeting. We have also established that with the help of psychoresource calculators, on average we wake up with a take-home psychoresource of between 40-60% to budget and utilise on any specific day. We have identified that spending is usually in three main areas: fixed, variable, and unexpected. Let's now take time to look at each in more detail. We should bear in mind that our psychological processes are never truly free of stress, even when we are happy and feel content. Happiness itself brings stress; an example is going on holiday. This is perceived as a pleasurable life event that most families look forward to. However, it is not a stress-free experience and requires organisation, preparation, punctuality, and adjustment to a new environment and possibly a new time zone. Other examples include a wedding, childbirth, or something as simple as going for dinner with friends. The point we need to understand is that every event exposes our psychological processes to some degree of stress. As a matter of fact, life is a continuous chain reaction of events; hence we can never be totally free of stress.

Fixed Psychoresource Spending

Experiencing constant stress of some degree gradually consume our psychoresource. Hypothetically speaking, one can take an example of a parked car with a running engine. Leaving your car running for a few hours will not be hugely detrimental to your fuel tank- insignificant perhaps- but there will be a degree of energy consumption. A similar principle applies to our psychological systems; they operate continuously with no shutting down. Constant use results in psychoresource expenditure that is not significant in the short term, but significant in the long term hence it has a cumulative effect. For example, if a car is left with the engine running the whole night, one is likely to notice some fuel reduction the following morning by just looking at the fuel bar. This is termed our fixed psychoresource spend. It is unavoidable; we are all required to live with it and accept it.

Fixed psychoresource spending could be permanent as is the case with childhood trauma, the effects of which typically remain with an individual for life. A significant life event such as the loss of a loved one emotionally scars an individual forever, irrespective of the fact that the intensity may well reduce over time; the subjective loss lives on.

Another example is acquired permanent disability. If the condition is unlikely to improve then even after adapting and adjusting to a changed lifestyle and priorities, it will continue to cause a baseline level of distress that will continue to consume one's psychoresource. If one does not have fixed employment due to chronic ill health for example, psychoresource spend could still be high since the form and nature of activities generating the stress may be different but not the degree of constant stress.

Fixed psychoresource spending could be time limited. This includes raising a young family. As an example, consider someone who is employed in a busy job, drives a car to work 30 miles a day, has a wife who also works, and they have 2 young children who are looked after by their grandmother when both parents are at work. Just imagine the level of mental activity generated by this family starting from the moment they wake up, get ready for work, get the children ready for school, drive to school, drop them off, drive to work and deal with the ongoing stresses. This is in addition to reliance on grandparents who may find it a struggle to look after the children after school, ensuring they are fed and settled for bed by the time the parents return home. The individuals would feel exhausted and subdued at the thought of having to do it all again the following day. Imagine the level of psychoresource spend of everyone in this household collectively. But this will be time limited since children are expected to grow up and to start taking responsibilities gradually and after some years stress is not as intense hence the psychoresource spend is less.

Variable Psychoresource Spending

This spend is directly proportional to our level of mental activity, much like financial spend. If we chose to partake in a busy day full of activities, there will be more spend in a similar way financial spend would be greater the longer you browsed a shopping mall. Conversely, if we undertake fewer activities, our variable spend will be less.

Unpredictability breeds variability. A volatile domestic environment with a high risk of unpredictable arguments, places sudden and unplanned demands on an individual's psychoresource hence psychoresource spending is very much variable under these uncertain conditions.

Balancing financial needs and remaining within budget during these times of ever-changing costs of living is, in itself a source of variable psychoresource spending. A particularly hard day at work, an argument with the local shopkeeper or even failing to catch the right train on time could all be responsible for variable psychoresource spend.

Variable psychological spending carries the risk of pushing us into psychodebt more than fixed psychoresource spending and even more so than psychoresource taxation (which was deducted by our mind at the base). We can likely assume that the vast majority of people in the world suffering from psychoresource debt or psychodebt, do so as a direct result of variable psychoresource spending. This is because it is very hard to budget for unexpected variability in life.

Unexpected Psychoresource Spending

The third section of psychoresource budgeting addresses unexpected spending. Let us look at some examples before going into detail. Consider the loss of a loved one. Even if the individual is prepared for the bereavement and loss (for example this may be expected of an elderly relative who was suffering from a terminal illness) it is still perceived as a shock to the psychological process and requires substantial resources to deal with. In cases of sudden and unexpected death, substantially more resources will be required especially when coping with the loss of a child or young adult.

Another example is relationship breakdown. Just imagine your partner turns around and brings the relationship to an end by saying, "I no longer love you". In this case, even if the relationship was rocky for a while and it was not expected to last for long, this life event requires substantial psychoresources to keep oneself composed. If the break-up is sudden and the relationship was well established, one would feel like a tree whose roots had been torn from the ground by heavy winds. The question is whether any of us carry the required resources in their psychobank for immediate access? The answer is probably no. In these situations, most of us are left with the only option of "spend now, pay later" and we resort to borrowing on our psychocredit card with a high interest rate.

There are plenty of unexpected life events which can place our psychological systems to the test including witnessing a crime, a car accident, robbery, an accident at home causing temporary or permanent physical disability and the list goes on.

Signs and Symptoms of Psychoruptcy

We have reached a stage where we have acquired the concepts of psychoresource budgeting, psychotax, psychocurrency, psychocredit and the availability of psychoresource for us to use on a typical day. Now is an ideal time to identify the risk factors for and signs of psychoruptcy. Recognizing these crucial warning signs may just save you from proceeding down the slippery slope of psychodebt towards psychoruptcy!

As the saying goes "the eyes don't see what the mind doesn't know". If we know what signs and symptoms could be indicative of psychoresource debt or psychodebt, we will be able to establish the extent of the debt. Furthermore, with effective debt management, it is possible for one to acquire additional psychoresources to recover and be able to save resources for unexpected future life events. In theory, this is very similar to financial debt management, the difference being that financial debt can easily be seen in numbers, whereas with psychological debt we cannot see our emotions- we can only feel them. Thus, the signs and symptoms of psychodebt are not seen but felt. It is important that we can recognize these on time.

One such sign is an observed change in an individual's demeanor and presentation. Others are likely to notice the difference, but the individual themself might not have the insight- at least not to begin with. The possible signs could include low level frustration, irritability, social avoidance, short-temperedness, forgetfulness, lack of interest in day-to-day activities, and an overall motivational compromise whereby everything feels like an effort. Another set of symptoms could include changes to our basic biological functions, which are essential in keeping us afloat both physically and mentally. For example, a good night's sleep is a must. Any change in an individual's sleep pattern, especially difficulty falling asleep, is indicative of psychodebt. Sleep is integral to our wellbeing. During sleep our brain recharges for the following day. If we don't give the brain sufficient rest, it quickly loses its battle against the mind, which then enters a state of revenge. The mind's revenge is to charge us more psychotax, leaving less for us to spend and this, in turn reduces our ability to cope with typical day-to-day events, which now seem like huge inconveniences. To keep our mind rational and to ensure the brain's victory over the mind, we must sleep (and eat) well. If sleep is disturbed, we are simply in a state of psychoresource debt.

The other necessary element is our interest in food. Loss of interest in food- not necessarily a reduction in the quantity of food consumed- rather a loss of enthusiasm and passion for food, can indicate that psychodebt is fast approaching. This is a subtle sign that should not be ignored.

A reduction in our interest in the physical aspect of our romantic relationship is another sign that our mind is in a state of psychodebt. The romantic part of us concerned with love is likely to be affected immediately after (or in many cases, at the same time as) sleep and appetite deteriorate.

It is necessary to look for other signs as well; the digestive system may change its smooth working and we may end up experiencing episodes of constipation or diarrhea for no apparent reason. It is also possible that we start noticing that some foods are not getting properly digested and this may well change our dietary pattern.

Physical health investigations are likely to indicate that nothing is significantly wrong, and the associated stress may even increase our psychodebt. We may be short tempered, we may start experiencing nervous energy of unknown origin and at times, fear of impending threat when no such threat exists. We are likely to feel sad as if we are carrying the weight of the world on our shoulders as extra baggage. At this stage, we are in serious psychodebt and possibly, close to psychoruptcy!

Reversing Psychodebt

The reality is that there are many people in the world living life with psychodebt and many of them are close to psychoruptcy. Can we empower them to help themselves? Good news, the answer is a resounding yes! Any stage of psychodebt is reversible subject to the application of appropriate strategies and a basic understanding of how to enhance psychoresources. The latter can be achieved by either paying less tax to mind at the base or by effective management of your variable spending. We have established that fixed psychoresource spending is not good but unavoidable and we have no control over unexpected psychoresource spending because it is beyond our operational strength. The only room to maneuver is to effectively manage our variable psychoresource spending. Couple this with gaining greater control over our mind to deduct less tax from our original entitlement of 100% psychoresource at the start of each new day, and we are winning! Let us look at the practical steps we can take to achieve both results; pay less tax to mind as this will automatically increase our take-home psychosalary and effective management of variable psychoresource spending.

Before pressing the red button to reboot our system, we must realise that this will initially shut down the psychoresource center before restarting it again. This simply means that the initial days when change is implemented, will be extraordinarily hard, and one needs to be well prepared to fight the challenge. Keep in mind that nothing in life is easy; every change no matter how small it might be, exposes us to a challenge. There are plenty of examples around us and in our own lives: marriage, divorce, change in employment, moving house, just to name a few. It is reasonable to expect the phase of readjustment to be testing.

First and foremost, we need to enforce a measure of control over our domineering and lazy minds. It is likely the mind has already done damage by contributing towards you acquiring psychodebt in the first place and you do not want it to continue behaving like a bull in a china shop. It is crucial that we learn to exercise some level of control over it, even partially.

In real life, if someone does not listen to us, what do we do? We raise our voice and there are occasions when we even argue; we have certainly all seen people shouting and screaming at each other to make their point clear. Whether we like it or not, we must use the same strategy to bring our minds under control. We can start by slowly negotiating with our mind, try to convince it to stop pulling us down and stop running its own reel of tragic past events through our mind, which is unhelpful. We can strongly request the mind to stop sending us negative messages and only engage with positive mental dialogue.

In the first instance, your mind will refuse to listen to any argument you present it with. Your mind has spent years controlling you. Have you encountered anybody in the real world who is happy to hand over their control? Not at all! So how can you expect your mind to? If you start talking to your mind gently, in a civilized manner, it is likely that your mind will not listen, forcing you to raise your voice. This requires us to stand in front of the mirror, look into our eyes and say out loud that we refuse to let our mind win. Our mind resides in our brain, which is just an organ over which we have control- like every other organ in the body. This needs to be a daily exercise or repeated several times a day, to keep our mind in check and to progress through the remainder of the concept.

The next stage is to instruct your mind to reward you. How you do this is very simple. Typically, after doing a good deed, we fail to celebrate our actions and as the moment passes, we forget about the good we have done. Our minds, being inherently lazy fail to switch on our reward system so we do not feel content nor happy. Instead of dismissing the good deed- irrespective of how simple it may be, for example switching off the tap when brushing our teeth or choosing to add something healthier to our diet- we must explicitly acknowledge that good deed by saying it out loud. In doing so, the deed will be formally noted by our mind, which will then be obliged to activate our reward system, thereby making us feel better. Goodness is inbuilt in us, and this method will ensure that good deeds make us feel better. It is important to make it a habit to tell our minds on each occasion throughout the day that we have done good. Exercising the mind by consciously activating the reward center to initiate feeling happy and proud is key.

Regaining control over and exercising our mind serves to reduce our variable psychoresource spend and to generate greater psychocurrency. The latter can also be achieved by completing a powerful self-reflection exercise designed solely for the individual affected by the psychodebt. It is a highly personal and individual exercise that enables us to essentially rediscover ourselves. To facilitate this process, we will apply the 'Rule of 3'.

The Rule of 3

Ideally find a quiet space where you can be on your own with some paper and a pen. Identify and write down the following:

- Three of your strengths
- Three big wishes you would like granted
- Three changes you would like to bring into your life
- Three areas of your life you are prepared to compromise.

It is important that you progress through the above requests in the specific order in which they are listed. However, tempting it may be, avoid moving onto the next stage until the one before is completed. Take your time and work at your own pace. Being honest with yourself is key. This list carefully guides you through a process of self-reflection that enables you to optimize the growth of your psychoresource. Some parts of the process will be more challenging than others but persevere to the end to achieve a state of psychowealth.

Your Strengths

Identifying three strengths may be challenging for some, particularly those whose mind desperately tries to convince them that they have none. In most cases the automatic answer is "I don't know", which is understandable. When one has spent many years enslaved by the mind, it is very hard to think in any other way. We are all born full of potential with qualities that you may never believe you could possess. Trust me, you have many strengths, far in excess of three. It will take time to contemplate your top three strengths but be patient with yourself and do not give up; you are at battle with your mind and have no choice but to win.

If your mind tricks you into thinking about your weaknesses, then it might be helpful to acknowledge that everyone has weaknesses, it is part of being human. Then try to refocus on the task at hand-identifying your strengths. A word of advice whenever you find yourself reflecting on your weaknesses; try to come from a place of compassion (ask yourself "what do I often need support with?") rather than from a place of self-criticism ("what am I awful at?"). It is more constructive and less damaging to one's self-esteem.

Big Wishes

The next stage invites you to write down your three big wishes. Here you have the freedom to identify and express what you truly desire in life. You have permission to throw caution to the wind, to shake loose your constraints and let your imagination run wild! Your wishes do not need to be achievable nor realistic, but they must come from the heart. There is something magical about our wildest wishes. They are a window into our dreams and fantasies, which in turn offer us insight into our needs and hopes. They motivate us to consider our own potential for growth.

Try to envision what your ideal life would look like. Removing ourselves from reality for the purpose of this exercise might feel strange, like we are entering unfamiliar territory. It might prove difficult for some as rarely do people take the time to explore what it is they really want, often they are unsure. For others the break from reality is a welcome relief, albeit temporary. Imagining an alternative, better life can prompt us to start a dialogue with ourselves about creating a more positive future. Ironically, the last person in the world we make an effort to get to know is *ourself!*

Manifesting Change

The next stage is to commit to introducing 3 changes into your life. This is an opportunity for you to make an active contribution towards winning the battle against your own mind. These changes need to be both realistic and achievable; to begin with keep them small and simple so you avoid setting yourself up for failure and you can manage your expectations. Over time as we gradually acquire large reserves of psychowealth we can afford to set ourselves more ambitious goals and attempt to establish bigger changes.

In addition to behavioural changes such as adopting a healthier diet or going for a daily morning walk, one can also target physical appearance including the following: dress sense, hair style, use of make-up. All these changes are valid as long as you are able to adhere to them in the long-term.

You might not realise this but establishing even the smallest change equates to a significant win in terms of reclaiming control over your mind. It takes courage to challenge the mind and this simple exercise will enable you to experience success in doing so, which gives you the momentum to continue confronting the mind. Furthermore, it will demonstrate that you are not as helpless or powerless as you might feel. The idea of introducing change may have been unthinkable just a few days ago!

Life Compromises

Now you have reached the final stage which involves identifying three aspects of your life that you are prepared to compromise. It is universally known that in life we simply cannot "have it all". Life is a sequence of trade-offs. We cannot enjoy the advantages of single life and be married. We cannot have a busy weekend and get lots of rest. You cannot be a leader and have little responsibility. It is one way or the other.

Some trade-offs are unavoidable and out of our control, these include: the choice of our parents, the environment in which we are raised as children, availability of resources at birth and many more. The type of trade-off with which we are concerned, are those that require a conscious choice or decision on our part. Those that require us to weigh out the good and the bad and commit to a particular path. An example is choosing to remain with your life partner despite feeling unsatisfied in order to provide the children with a stable family unit for as long as possible. Another example is to tolerate employment one really hates as it provides a much-needed salary. If we examine our own lives, will realise the extent to which we rely on these trade-offs and the number of compromises we must accept on a daily basis. The list will be never-ending. This is the case for everyone, you are not alone!

The attitude that life is a series of trade-offs, brings with it an unexpected sense of relief and freedom. If we can accept that we do not have to have everything for it to be good then we can more readily reach a compromise with less grief, frustration, resentment, and disappointment (all of which can be paralyzing) that we may be "missing out" on something else. We can appreciate the chosen path for all the good it has to offer and feel content.

Another key to navigating compromise is balance. Life is best when we avoid living it according to "all or nothing" thinking; such extremes in thinking are dangerous. Compromises are most successful when we consider a mixture of both our needs and desires and not one or the other. The aim is to reach a happy equilibrium of the two. Sometimes the distinction between needs and desires is confused. To clarify, needs refer to an individual's basic requirements that must be fulfilled to survive, for example food and sleep. They are a necessity and tend to be limited in number and remain constant over time. Desires describe what an individual would like, their preferences, for example wealth and power. These are likely to change over time and lack of fulfillment can result in disappointment but not death. We all have needs and desires; get good at differentiating between the two and strike a balance.

Secrets to Psychowealth

By now you have managed to achieve partial control over your mind and have started paying off your psychodebt. The final stage of this therapeutic process is to use all the elements you have identified in conjunction with each other. When you look at your answers collectively, you will be surprised to see the coordination between them all. This indicates that only a few basic changes in your life are needed to be psychologically wealthy.

Three guiding principles to challenge the mind and acquire a state of psychowealth are as follows:

- Focus on your strengths.
- Achieve a realistic and logical balance between your wishes and needs.

- Focus on bringing change into your life (but do not concern yourself with changing others).

This is a life-long exercise and a skill that once learned, should never be forgotten because who would want to return to a miserable psychodebt-ridden life when you have the tools to enjoy the life of a psychomillionaire!

30

Generating Psychowealth

The Rule of 3

- Complete the steps in the order listed
- Be patient & honest with yourself
- Persevere & don't give up
- You got this!

Step 1
3 STRENGTHS

Step 2
3 BIG WISHES

Step 3
3 CHANGES TO INTRODUCE

Step 4
3 COMPROMISES

9 798848 633917